To Hell
with the Diet

*A Feast of Quotations
for the Guilty Epicurian*

Aubrey Malone

The
History
Press

First published 2014

The History Press
The Mill, Brimscombe Port
Stroud, Gloucestershire, GL5 2QG
www.thehistorypress.co.uk

British Library Cataloguing in Publication Data.
A catalogue record for this book is available from the British Library.

ISBN 978 1 84588 832 9

Typesetting and origination by The History Press
Prnted in Great Britain

Contents

Why You Shouldn't Diet

Don't diet – all you'll lose is your sanity.

John Candy

Women should try to increase their size rather than decrease it. The bigger we are, the more space we'll take up and the more we'll have to be reckoned with.

Roseanne

Don't ever forget: 75 per cent of the word 'diet' is 'die'.

Ruth Bryant

The whole of nature is a conjugation of the verb 'to eat'.

William Inge

We're not designed to ingest 150 different varieties of vitamins each day, to wear down our knee joints by jogging miles and miles each week, to get up at the crack of dawn to do our keep fit exercises, to conquer the corporate Mount Everest at breakfast time, to notch up more sexual conquests than Don Juan during his prime. Does that symbol of all we hold dear, the British bulldog, worry about additives in its food, impressing its neighbours, making friends and influencing people? No, it just wants a warm home, a generous provider and to be left to its own devices between meals.

Rosemary Barr

It took a lot of willpower but I finally gave up trying to diet.

Louis Safian

No diet will remove all the fat from your body because
the brain is entirely fat. Without a brain you might
look good, but all you could do is run for public office.

George Bernard Shaw

Fat people don't seem to age as much as thin ones,
not when you get up close and inspect the damage.

Hunter Davies

Fat generally tends to make a man a better
husband. His wife is happy in the knowledge she's
not married to a woman-chaser. Few fat men
chase girls because they get winded so easily.

Hal Boyle

Dieting can't work. The pleasant habits of
eating and drinking were never meant to
be subject to a chemical equation.

Lord Horder

I need starch and sweets and alcohol because
I enjoy them. I'm damned if I'm going to upset my
metabolism and thereby my happiness by straining
after a youthful line. If my nerves are cosily enclosed
in enough fatty tissue to keep them from twitching,
the people near me are also more likely to be happy.
I would really rather be fat than disagreeable.

Noel Coward

Man's chief difference from brutes lies in the exuberant excess of his subjective propensities. Prune his extravagance, sober him and you undo him.

William James

The worst thing about most diets is that they lower the amount of food you're supposed to ingest.

Robert Morley

I know a man who gave up smoking, drinking, sex and rich food. He was healthy right up to the day he killed himself.

Johnny Carson

I don't want my girl to be so skinny she can knife me with her knee.

Mark Twain

Get some food into this man.
You can't lead a country at 176 pounds.

Marlon Brando on John F. Kennedy after they both weighed themselves together; Brando came in at 187 pounds

Today's beauty ideal, strictly enforced by the media, is a person with the same level of body fat as a paperclip. By such standards, Marilyn Monroe was an oil tanker.

Dave Barry

It seems the only way to have a healthy life nowadays
is not to eat. Starve to death. At least when you're
dying you'll know it isn't of anything serious.

Dave Allen

Thin people are beautiful but fat ones are adorable.

Jackie Gleason

To ask women to become unnaturally thin is
to ask them to relinquish their sexuality.

Naomi Wolf

There are now more overweight people
in America than average weight people,
so overweight people are now average.

Jay Leno

There was only one occasion in my life when I put
myself on a strict diet and I can tell you, hand on heart,
it was the most miserable afternoon I have ever spent.

Denis Norden

I'm a hypochondriac. When I go on a diet and lose
weight, I think there's something wrong with me.

Don Rickles

Why do people who work in health
shops always look so unhealthy?

Victoria Wood

I think it's really sad that a lot of women think 'If I lose half a stone everything will be perfect'. It won't. Everything will be exactly the same. You'll just be a bit thinner.

Lorraine Kelly

Eating is our earliest metaphor, preceding our consciousness of gender difference, race, nationality and language. We eat before we talk.

Margaret Atwood

The first part of the body to lose weight in a fashionable diet is the brain.

Peter Gray

A woman's body is in competition with every other female body on the planet as regards avoirdupois ... and 99 per cent of the time she's going to lose.

Serena Gray

There are an awful lot of skinny people in the cemetery.

Beverly Sills

Diets don't suit me. I got addicted to the menu.

Mort Sahl

I've started to diet. I'm still a slob, but now I'm a thin slob.

Peter Dobereiner

Life is too damn short and food too damn good to
waste time trying to convince folks that I'm worthy of
respect simply because the day the good Lord chose
to pass out extra helpings of hips and ass.

Mo'Nique

All a diet means for a man is that he eats oatmeal ...
as well as everything else he always ate.

E.W. Howe

I'm so neurotic that I worry I'm going to
lose weight when I go on a diet.

Grace Malloy

I like a man with a paunch.

Sandra Bullock

An elegant degree of plumpness is peculiar
to the skin of the softer sex.

Edward Hogarth

Slim women may look slick but a fat
woman stays. Ask any corset manufacturer.

Lennie Lower

When you buy two Big Macs for two bucks,
it becomes cost efficient to be a fat bastard.

Jim Wyatt

The ingredients for anorexia are:
1 cup low self-esteem, 2 cups self-control, ¼ cup
determination, 1½ cups strength, ½ cup solitude,
2 tbsp routine, 3 tbsp secrecy and lies, 2tsp jealousy,
3 tsp guilt, a dash of anger and 1 cup tears.

Internet entry

Let me have men around me who are fat.

William Shakespeare

I'm fat and proud of it. If someone asks me how my
diet is going, I say 'Fine – how was your lobotomy?'

Roseanne

I'm quite convinced that in about ten or twenty years'
time when you buy food, it will have a message on it
saying 'Warning: Food is Dangerous to Your Health'.

Dave Allen

When I was at my thinnest a few years ago I was
miserable. Now I've put a lot of the weight back
on and I'm comfortable with who I am. My real
self is someone who eats too many pies. It doesn't
mean I'm secretly crying out for help.

Vanessa Feltz

Dieting makes you fat.

Geoffrey Cannon

There's no use going on a diet if you have to
starve yourself to death to live longer.

Colin Greene

Dieting results from television and radio ads
that have made it seem wicked to cast a shadow.
The emaciated look appeals to some women, though
not too many men. They're seldom seen pinning
up a *Vogue* illustration in a machine shop.

Peg Bracken

I feel about aeroplanes the way I feel about diets.
They're wonderful things for other people to go on.

Jean Kerr

Not for me the heresies of healthy eating favoured by
Edwina Currie, or the hypochondriacal fears of cholesterol.

Lord Hailsham

Women are born to be well-rounded and
soft. Children love to snuggle into big-breasted
women and so do most men.

Erin Pizzey

I've never followed a diet, never bought a diet
book, never counted a calorie. Life's too short.
I could go to sleep on a bed of mashed potato.

Graham Norton

No one ever became a success in the
world without a large bottom.

Adam Sedgwick

I hate skinny women, especially when they say things
like 'Sometimes I forget to eat'. I've forgotten my
mother's maiden name, I've forgotten my car keys, but
you've got to be a special kind of stupid to forget to eat.

Marsha Warfield

Nothing in the world arouses more false
hopes than the first four hours of a diet.

Nora Ephron

I once went to one of those diet places to get in shape.
Six hundred calories a day and decaf. Ugh!

Bette Davis

Most diets are crap.

Anne Diamond

2

Exercising
(... One's Right Not To)

The only exercise I take is walking behind
the coffins of friends who exercise.

Peter O'Toole

Exercise is the yuppie version of bulimia.

Barbara Ehrenreich

I'm not a workout guy. I walk and I smoke. That's
about it. I'm a softball guy. Softball is just baseball
with beer. That's why they make the ball so big –
so you can see it when you're shit-faced.

Denis Leary

I'm not into working out. My philosophy is:
no pain, no pain.

Carol Liefer

I exercise daily to keep my figure. I keep patting
my hand against the bottom of my chin. It works
too. I have the thinnest fingers in town.

Totie Fields

My idea of a good workout is two hours spent
worrying about the bags under my eyes.

Maureen Lipman

My favourite form of exercise? Standing up.

Jackie Gleason

Whenever I feel like exercise,
I lie down until the feeling passes.

Robert Hutchins

I get all my exercise on the golf course. Whenever
I see my friends collapse, I run for the paramedics.

Red Skelton

Show me a man who jogs every morning
and I'll show you a breaking marriage.

Kenneth Robinson

Jogging is for people who aren't intelligent
enough to watch breakfast TV.

Victoria Wood

I get a lot of exercise. Last week I was
out seven nights running.

Jackie Gleason

Walking isn't a lost art. One must, by some
means, get to the garage.

Evan Esar

I'm very religious. I refuse to workout on
any week that has a Sunday in it.

John Candy

The best reducing exercise is to shake the head violently from side to side when offered a second helping.

Kay Finch

Do I lift weights? Sure, every time I stand up.

Dolly Parton

Exercise is bunk. If you're healthy you don't need it and if you're sick you shouldn't take it.

Henry Ford

I don't workout. If God had wanted us to bend over He'd put diamonds on the floor.

Joan Rivers

I often take exercise. Why, only yesterday I had breakfast in bed.

Oscar Wilde

I love watching keep-fit videos while munching chocolate chip cookies.

Dolly Parton

The way I exercise is by stumbling and then falling into a coma.

Oscar Levant

I'm really fitter than most people because when
I run it's like I have to carry two children on my back.

Jo Brand

The only exercise programme that ever worked for
me was getting up in the morning and jogging my
memory to remind myself how much I hate to exercise.

Dennis Miller

I'd rather lie on a sofa than sweep beneath it.

Shirley Conran

I don't jog. If I die I want to be sick.

Abe Lemmons

There's too much rubbish talked about exercise.
Sloth is the key to life. Every morning when
I get up it's 'Up down, one, two, three.'
And then the same for the other eyelid.

Les Dawson

If God meant us to touch our toes, He would
have put them further up our body.

Jenny Eclair

I've been doing leg lifts faithfully for about fifteen years.
The only thing that's gotten thinner is the carpet.

Rita Rudner

The two best exercises in the world are making love
and dancing but a simpler one is to stand on tiptoe.

Barbara Cartland

I'm pushing sixty. That's enough exercise for me.

Mark Twain

Cricket is the only game that you can
actually put on weight when playing.

Tommy Docherty

I like yoga. I enjoy any exercise where you get
to lie down on the floor and then go to sleep.

Rita Rudner

If God had wanted us to run, instead of a bellybutton
He'd have given us a fast forward one.

Joe Hickman

If my hangover isn't too bad I do sit-ups.

Hugh Grant

Fun Run – now there's an oxymoron.

Joe Bennett

My favourite exercise is the refrigerator
lunge, followed by the microwave push.

Andy Rhoads

My favourite machine at the gym is the vending machine.

Caroline Rhea

I have a punishing workout regime. Every day I do
three minutes on a treadmill. Then I lie down,
drink a glass of vodka and smoke a cigarette.

Anthony Hopkins

Taking the lock off my freezer is the only exercise I get.

Marlon Brando

The only way I would ever do sit-ups is if someone
put the remote control between my toes.

Dolly Parton

Let's not allow exercise bikes to catapult us
back to the days of the buttless monkeys.

Lisa Carver

My doctor told me to exercise.
He said walking would get me into shape.
'I already have a shape,' I told him. 'It's round.'

Brendan Grace

If God had meant us to walk everywhere
He wouldn't have given us Little Chefs.

Bernice Woodall

What would you call an aerobics instructor who
doesn't cause pain and agony? Unemployed.

Michael Hargreaves

According to a study of health clubs, men sweat
more than women. Well, sure. It takes a lot
more effort to hold in their gut for an hour.

Jay Leno

My favourite exercise is walking a block and a half to
the corner store to buy fudge. Then I call a cab to get
back home. There's no need to overdo anything.

Ellen DeGeneres

Do I exercise? Well I once jogged to the ashtray.

Will Self

The only athletic sport I ever mastered was backgammon.

Douglas Jerrold

The only thing I've ever been able to jump to is a
conclusion, and even that leaves me out of breath.

G.K. Chesterton

Exercise is a short cut to the cemetery.

John Mortimer

He used to be an all-round athlete. Now he's just all round.

Henny Youngman

My wife is doing Pilates. At least I think that's his name.

Peter Sasso

The trouble with jogging is that by the time you realise you're not in shape for it, it's too far to walk back.

Franklin P. Jones

The main way I keep fit is by wrestling with my conscience.

Spike Milligan

I smoke 100 cigarettes a day.
Coughing is the only exercise I get.

Bill Hicks

The best exercise I get these days is rolling my oxygen tank around like a beach ball when I get out of bed.

Marlon Brando

I like long walks – especially when they're taken by people who annoy me.

Fred Allen

Exercise is only for people who get paid to do it.

Bette Davis

I'm not fit. It takes me ten minutes to catch my
breath after climbing the stairs. I don't like walking.
I have a taxi account I spend my millions on.

Maeve Binchy

Everybody's lazy these days. The other morning I had to
shout to the wife twice to come upstairs and dress me.

Les Dawson

If God wanted me to touch my toes
He would have put them on my knees.

Roseanne Barr

My wife lost two stones swimming last year.
I should have tied them tighter round her.

Les Dawson

After breakfast I exercise. This girl called Frances
usually comes to my house. I pay this poor bitch
to come in and just push me around. We exercise
together, which means she does a lot of exercise
and I do a lot of 'Oh please, Frances, not today.'

Joan Rivers

I don't exercise and because I'm happy
I eat and eat, mainly junk food.

Charlotte Church

I had a stalker but he left me. He got fed up
waiting for me to leave the house.

Jo Brand

Why did the aerobics instructor cross the road?
Because somebody on the other side could still walk.

Joe O'Shea

Better to have loafed and lost than
never to have loafed at all.

James Thurber

Every morning it takes so much out of me trying to sit
up that I end up falling asleep again after the exertion.

Roscoe 'Fatty' Arbuckle

I'd rather wear black in August than do one sit-up.

Joy Behar

I'd like to force-feed supermodels with chocolate
eclairs and keep them tied up so they couldn't
exercise. It's much easier to make them look
like you than try to look like them.

Jo Brand

I try to keep fit. I've got these parallel bars at home. I run
at them and try to buy a drink from both of them.

Arthur Smith

People tell me I look good at 64. I don't know what
my secret is. I don't go to the gym, I don't train and
I'm not that careful about what I eat. The best advice
I can give anyone is to choose your parents wisely.

Harrison Ford

Before I jog I have to do one thing:
check the infrastructure of the road.

Jo Brand

I believe sleeping less leads to big guts.
So when a man is napping on the couch
he can tell his wife he's working out.

Jay Leno

The only weights I lift are my dogs.

Olivia Newton-John

What do I do to stay fit? Passing the vodka bottle.

Keith Richards

It was such a lovely day I thought it was a pity to get up.

Somerset Maugham

Here's a reason to smile:
every seven minutes of every day,
someone in an aerobics class pulls a hamstring.

Robin Williams

I do the Peter Fonda workout, not the Jane one. In other words I wake up, take a hit of acid, smoke a joint and then run round to my sister's house looking for money.

Kevin Meaney

I believe every human has a finite number of heartbeats. I don't intend to waste any of mine running around exercising.

Neil Armstrong

Researchers are now saying wine helps you lose weight. It's not the actual wine though; it's all the walking around you do trying to find your car.

Jay Leno

The toughest part of professional snooker is getting up and down from the chair. It really makes your leg muscles ache. To stop the pain I do skipping and a press-up, or two press-ups before a big match.

Steve Davis

If it weren't for the fact that the TV set and the refrigerator are so far apart, some of us wouldn't get any exercise at all.

Joey Adams

3

Pills, Operations
and Doctors

The last man in the world whose opinion
I would take on what to eat would be a doctor.
It is far safer to consult a waiter,
and not a bit more expensive.

Robert Lynd

The first need in the reform of hospital
management is the death of all dieticians
and the resurrection of the French chef.

Martin Fischer

I told my doctor I get very tired when I go on a diet
so he gave me pep pills. The result? I just ate faster.

Joe E. Lewis

I once got hit by a Volkswagen.
I had to go to the hospital to have it removed.

Pat McCormick

I had a tummy tuck before liposuction came in.
They took three pounds of fat off. Actually it was
mayonnaise, mashed potatoes and gravy.

Phyllis Diller

At fat farms and beauty spas, one pays astronomical
sums to be over-exercised and underfed.

Peg Bracken

I joined a health club last year which cost me
a fortune but I still didn't lose any weight.
Apparently you have to turn up.

Hal Roach

Why go to the gym when you can relax
unconscious under a skilled surgeon's knife?

Jenny Eclair

I've joined a Keep Fat Club.
Every Wednesday morning we meet and
eat as many cakes as we can manage.

Jo Brand

The cardiologist's diet goes like this:
If it tastes good, spit it out.

John Goodman

I told the doctor I had a terrible stomach problem.
She said, 'You have. It's bloody enormous.'

Jo Brand

An obese woman went to her doctor for advice.
He told her to eat normally for a day, then skip a
day, then eat normally again, and so on. She came
back to him after a week, having lost two stone.
'How do you feel?' he asked her. 'Terrible,' she said.
'I've been skipping so much my legs are numb'.

Sheena Love

As for butter versus margarine,
I trust cows more than chemists.

Joan Gussow

Psychologists argue that eating disorders are caused
by upbringing – specifically the bringing up of your lunch.

Debbie Bareham

My doctor told me jogging
could add years to my life. I told him,
'Yeah, since I began I already feel ten years older.'

Lee Trevino

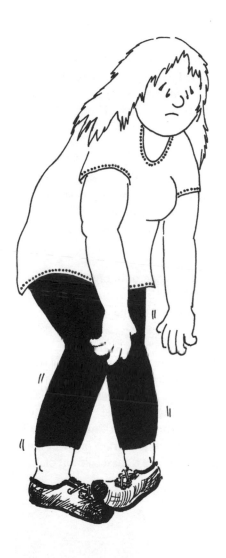

After *One Flew Over the Cuckoo's Nest* people thought a
psychiatric ward was a place where an evil and sadistic
person humiliated depressed people. This is actually
a more accurate description of Weight Watchers.

Jo Brand

I'd love it if there was a pill to make me thin.
I'd take one to bring me down to six stone
and then eat my way up to ten.
What a weekend that would be.

Jo Brand

I've never gone to a doctor in my adult life,
feeling instinctively that doctors either
meant cutting or, just as bad, diet.

Carson McCullers

My doctor flipped the weight of the scale over
another notch, looked it me with annoyance
and said, 'Man does not live by bread alone'.
'You think I don't know that?' I replied. 'Any
fool knows you have to make it into a sandwich,
top it with homemade preserves or cover it with
cheese sauce and make a casserole out of it.'

Erma Bombeck

My doctor told me to do something that puts me
out of breath. So I've taken up smoking again.

Jo Brand

My doctor has advised me to give up those
intimate little dinners for four – unless there
are three other people eating with me.

Orson Welles

Sydney Smith was once told by his doctor
that he should walk on an empty stomach.
'Whose?' he replied.

Leonard Rossiter

Very well. Then please consider that I did not
come to consult you until tomorrow

*Johannes Brahms to his doctor, after having been
prescribed a strict diet he didn't like*

I went to the doctor. 'How do I stand?' I asked him.
He said, 'It's a bloody mystery to me.'

Les Dawson

I once thought of having the fat hoovered off me by a
doctor who does liposuction. I asked him how he managed
to suck the same amount off different parts of the body.
'I don't,' he said, 'You'll still be oddly shaped, but it will be
a thin odd shape, not a fat odd one like you have now.'

Orson Welles

A radio commercial says that a certain diet pill works
three times faster than starvation. Question: Are they
guessing or did they really run those tests?

George Carlin

The FDA has just approved pills that help
you lose weight by making you feel full.
The recommended dosage is 5,000 a day.

Conan O'Brien

Jackie Gleason had a big heart transplant in Chicago,
a five-hour operation. Four of these were spent
trying to get him on the operating table.

Bob Hope

I recently had my annual physical examination, which I get once every seven years. When the nurse weighed me, I was shocked to discover how much stronger the Earth's gravitational pull had become in that time.

Dave Barry

Plastic surgeons take the fat from your rear end and use it to bang out the dents in your face. It gives a whole new meaning to dancing cheek to cheek.

Anita Wise

4

The Hell of
Healthy Food

I didn't fight my way to the top of the
food chain to be a vegetarian.

Joe O'Herlihy

Parsley is gharsley.

Ogden Nash

God invented vegetables to let women
get even with their children.

P.J. O'Rourke

The local groceries are all out of broccoli, loccoli.

Roy Blount Jnr

Vulgarity is the garlic in the salad of taste.

Cyril Connolly

I can't bear salad. It grows while you're eating it.
You start on one side of your plate and by the
time you've got to the other there's a fresh crop
of lettuce taken root and sprouted up.

Alan Ayckbourn

Vegetables are interesting but lack a sense of purpose
unless accompanied by a good cut of meat.

Fran Lebowitz

A cucumber should be well sliced, dressed with
pepper and vinegar – and then thrown out.

Samuel Johnson

The only obvious advantage to being an
adult is that you can eat your dessert without
having sampled the vegetables.

Lisa Alther

There's somebody at every
dinner party who eats all the celery.

Kin Hubbard

Women who have a low-calorie lettuce leaf for
lunch will often have had enough snacks in the
morning to sustain a small Turkish weightlifter.

Guy Browning

Salad isn't food. Salad is slimy green
background for croutons.

Cynthia Heimel

Men only date thin girls because they're too
weak to argue. And salads are cheap.

Jennifer Fairbanks

I have no truck with lettuce, cabbage and similar
chlorophyll. Any dietician will tell you that
a running foot of apple strudel contains four
times the vitamins of a bushel of beans.

S.J. Perelman

I fantasise about scientists discovering
that lettuce is fattening.

Erma Bombeck

I never worry about diets. The only carrots that interest me are the ones you get in diamonds.

Mae West

Cooked carrots. On way to mouth, drop in lap. Then smuggle to garbage in napkin.

Delia Ephron

Most vegetarians I ever saw looked enough like their food to be classed as cannibals.

Finley Peter Dunne

If you want to ingratiate yourself with a gluttonous slob, take him/her out for a meal. Skip the nouvelle cuisine or any similar delicate food preparation. It may look pretty on the plate, with the tomatoes cut to look like roses, but no self-respecting slob could possibly be satisfied with such small portions of predominantly rabbit food.

Tracey Jeune

Last week I read about a diet that said 'Just eat half of everything you like.' I'm adhering to it diligently. Today I've eaten half a stick of celery, and half a pig.

Sally Jackson

A great many people in Los Angeles are on strict diets that restrict their intake of synthetic foods. The reason for this appears to be a widely-held belief that organically grown fruit and vegetables make the cocaine work faster.

Fran Lebowitz

You get as much actual food out of eating artichoke
as you would licking thirty postage stamps.

Miss Piggy

Broccoli, green beans and asparagus can only be
enjoyed by nerds, nuns and people with bowel disorders.

Dan Buckley

I have just given up spinach for Lent.

F. Scott Fitzgerald

I hate health food in general, really. What I hate the
most is those natural food shops. What is organic?
Just another word for dirty fruit, for God's sake.

Ruby Wax

Health food makes me sick.

Bob Monkhouse

Health foods give you a radish complexion

John Crosbie

Vegetarianism is harmless enough, though it is apt
to fill a man with wind and self-righteousness.

Robert Hutchinson

Vegetarians have wicked, shifty eyes and
laugh in a cold, calculating manner.
They favour beards, steal stamps
and pinch little children.

J.B. Morton

The first time I tried organic wheat bread
I thought I was chewing on roofing material.

Robin Williams

Shredded wheat tastes like sawdust covered with milk.

Ian Botham

Why is it that any food that doesn't cause
you to put on weight tastes like crap?

Jeff Heaney

I'm President of the United States and
I'm not going to eat any more broccoli.

George Bush in 1990

Eating tofu can reduce your
chances of catching certain diseases ...
but most people would prefer to catch the diseases.

Craig Kilborn

It's difficult to say anything nice about
broccoli except that it has no bones.

Johnny Martin

5

Favourite
Foods

What's my favourite food? Seconds.

John Candy

You don't have a man, you need spaghetti.

Oprah Winfrey

More than once I have been cured of
mild depression by baking a cake.

Josceline Dimbleby

How do I feel about edible panties?
Well if you're drunk enough and your teeth
are sharp enough, every panty is edible.

Brian McKim

What, no cheese?

Edward VII, after a ten-course meal

Roast beef, medium, is not only a food. It is a philosophy.

Edna Ferber

Man cannot live by bread alone;
he must have peanut butter.

James Garfield

Reality may not be the best of all possible worlds but it's
still the only place where you can get a decent steak.

Woody Allen

I like anything that comes under the heading,
'It's got calories and you can put it in your mouth'.

Jo Brand

Let them eat cake.

Marie Antoinette

He loves spaghetti more than me.

Luciano Pavarotti's wife

Oysters are more beautiful than any religion.

Saki

I left modelling because it's no fun trying to keep
yourself at 115 pounds when you like ice cream.

Kim Basinger

The Russians in World War II were enormously impressed
by Churchill at the table. His appetite for caviar and vodka
convinced them that they were fighting on the right side.

Robert Lewis Taylor

The noblest of all dogs is the hot dog.
It feeds the hand that bites it.

Laurence J. Peter

I wouldn't give somebody my last Rolo
if they were in a diabetic coma.

Jo Brand

Everything you see I owe to spaghetti.

Sophia Loren

My favourite animal is steak.

Erma Bombeck

I never met a calorie I didn't like.

Graffiti

The only safe pleasure for a parliamentarian
is a bag of boiled sweets.

Julian Critchley

Good mashed potato is one of the great luxuries
of life. I don't blame Elvis one bit for eating it
every night for the last years of his life.

Lindsey Bareham

I tried to commit suicide by putting my head
in the oven but there was a cake in it.

Lesley Boone

I love Thanksgiving turkey. It's the only time
in Los Angeles that you see natural breasts.

Arnold Schwarzenegger

If you have enough butter, anything is good.

Julia Childs

The only thing that tastes exactly like butter is butter.

Arthur Marshall

I love children if they're cooked properly.

W.C. Fields

Seeing snow for the first time, my grandson
jumped for joy and cried, 'Ooh, icing!'

Alex Lacey

No man is lonely while eating spaghetti.

Robert Morley

Dear Lord, I present these cookies to you as
an offering. If you wish me to eat them instead,
please give me no sign whatsoever. Thy will be done.

Homer Simpson

What would I like with my chips? More chips.

Roy 'Chubby' Brown

There's no such thing as a little garlic.

Arthur Baer

My favourite hobby is food.

John Candy

My husband's favourite food? Everything.

Hillary Clinton

One of the perks of being Vice President is you get
all the French fries the president can't get to.

Al Gore

I'm so hungry I could eat a pig's ass
through a tennis racquet.

Rosie O'Donnell

The worst drug today isn't smack or pot.
It's refined sugar.

George Hamilton

I like to evade the feminine stereotype. You say women
are afraid of mice? I'll show you. I'll eat the mouse.

Anne Beatts

Health food may be good for the conscience
but Oreos taste a hell of a lot better.

Robert Redford

I like the kind of food you need a forklift to eat.

Milton Berle

More pasta and less panache.

Mario Puzo

My idea of heaven would be eating pâté
de foie gras to the sound of trumpets.

Sydney Smith

I refuse to believe that trading recipes is silly.
Tuna fish casserole is at least as real as corporate stock.

Barbara Harrison

Irish coffee is the only drink that provides all four
essentials: alcohol, caffeine, sugar and fat.

Danny McGrath

My parents tried to stop me sucking my thumb
when I was a kid by putting mustard on it.
No wonder I'm a hot dog fan.

Jo Brand

My favourite book, movie and food is
Fried Green Tomatoes.

Jane Radcliffe

Our son has announced that he can't eat meat. What if
he starts wanting to save dolphins and says he has
to throw out all our tuna? I'm only saying this once:
I love my kids but I will never, ever give up my tuna.

Tim Taylor

Why is ranch dressing always ordered 'on the side'? It's the
mistress of salad dressing. Won't somebody stand up and
make a commitment to ranch dressing? Stop treating
her like a whore. Let her come with the salad to the
dinner party. Don't force her to drive in a separate car.

Ellen DeGeneres

I can't imagine living anywhere that I can't get a
corned-beef sandwich at three o'clock in the morning.

Rod Steiger

Poetry isn't the most important thing in life.
I'd much rather lie in a hot bath reading
Agatha Christie and sucking sweets.

Dylan Thomas

If people have to choose between friends and
sandwiches, they'll choose sandwiches.

Lord Boyd Orr

To the highly-stressed executive, a biro is a complete
meal. First you bend back the clip bit from the top
and bite it off. Then you mangle the top between your
teeth, suck out the little stopper and crunch away
at the pen itself. A standard biro counts towards
one of your five portions of fruit and veg per day.

Guy Browning

6

The Joy of
Chocolate

In Manhattan last month I heard a woman
borrowing the jargon of junkies to say to another
one, 'Want to do some chocolate?'

Diane Ackerman

Other things are just food but chocolate is chocolate.

Patrick Skene Catling

The best part of Easter is eating your children's candy
while they're sleeping and trying to convince them the
next morning that the chocolate rabbit came with one ear.

Anna Quindlen

I never met a chocolate I didn't like.

Deanna Troi

Thirteen out of every ten women prefer chocolate to maths.

Steven Scally

Be careful – chocolate can make your clothes shrink.

Ruby Wax

If they don't have chocolate in heaven, I'm not going.

Roseanne

Don't wreck a sublime chocolate experience by
feeling guilty. Chocolate isn't like premarital sex.
It will not make you pregnant.

Lora Brody

How can a two pound box of chocolates
make you gain ten pounds?

Roseanne

Just give me chocolate and no one gets hurt.

Joan Rivers

If in fact you are what you eat,
I am a 114-pound bar of bitter-sweet chocolate.

Lora Brody

Avoid any diet that discourages the use of hot fudge.

Rosie O'Donnell

Strength is the capacity to break a chocolate bar
into four pieces and then just eat one of them.

Judith Viorst

Nine out of ten people like chocolate.
The tenth person always lies.

John G. Tullius

I've lost a stone and a half in a month and three
days with Weight Watchers. I do it on the phone.
They run it rather like Alcoholics Anonymous.
You get a counsellor and you can call him
any time of the day or night if you're being
tempted by a packet of chocolate biscuits.

Robbie Coltrane

Women have a deeper and more complex relationship
with chocolate than they do with men. That's because
with chocolate you get more taste, more immediate
response, and you can also use your teeth.

Guy Browning

I like kinky sex with chocolate. I call it S&M&M.

Roseanne

With chocolate, as with most things,
the more calories the better.

Shelley Winters

Most chocolate chip cookies don't have
enough chocolate chips in them.

Judith Olney

Someone told me that giving up chocolate would reduce
my hot flushes. To be honest, I prefer the hot flushes.

Anna Granger

When Dad helped make a chocolate cake, the
kitchen ended up looking like Willy Wonka
had been murdered in there.

Robin Elms

Love is just a chocolate substitute.

Rosie O'Donnell

If you get melted chocolate all over your
hands, you're eating it too slowly.

Maureen Lipman

Chocolate isn't a substitute for love,
love is a substitute for chocolate.
Let's face it, it's much more reliable than a man.

Miranda Ingram

I once attempted to eat my body weight in
Belgian chocolate. After the first couple of kilos in
an art gallery the pictures seemed to be moving.
After a few more, in a chocolate haze, I heard the
voice of Tintin telling me to kill the Smurfs.

Ross Noble

It's in any film contract I make that the fridge in the
trailer is stacked sky-high with chocolate and cakes.

Dawn French

Office workers who've been shopping at lunchtime
like to store their food in the fridge until they can
take it home. That's fine, but don't ever take it out
of the carrier bag as there are men in every office
who believe that an unopened chocolate gateau
in the fridge was bought specifically for them.

Guy Browning

Flowers may speak the language of love
but it's chocolate that fans the flames.

Rebecca Pate

Like the final act of a play or the crescendo of a
symphony, we expect a good chocolate sweet to
leave us speechless, and craving for more.

Suzanne Ausnit

I'm a health food nut. But it can't be health
food with a chocolate outer coating.

Paula Poundstone

Why am I bothering to eat this chocolate?
I might as well apply it directly to my thighs.

Rhoda Morgenstern

I'd love to witness that virgin moment
when a baby first has chocolate.

Dawn French

Chocolate is the perfect food because the bliss factor
is exactly equal to the guilt factor and the colliding
of the two inside the brain uses so much energy
that the calories are completely cancelled out.

Cathy Guisemite

If I was a lesbian I could have chocolate cake for dinner
every night and still get laid. Men who have sex glands
in their eyes and centrefolds in their hearts are picky and
exacting about women's bodies. Other women are not.
Other women would be empathetic about cellulite.

Cynthia Heimel

He who lives without chocolate isn't worthy to live.

Jenny Eclair

I hate having kids with me at the supermarket;
the trolley is groaning with chocolate and biscuits –
and then *they* want something too.

Jo Brand

7

The Art of Cooking

Cooking is about not cheating yourself of pleasure.

Nigel Slater

The only saving grace of being at boarding school
was freedom from my mother's cooking.

Spike Hughes

My pet hate is nouvelle cuisine. The kitchen
staff stand back saying 'Enjoy, enjoy', and I find
myself staring in disbelief saying 'Find, find'.

Chris Tarrant

I'm not saying my kitchen is a religious
place, but if I were a voodoo princess I would
conduct my religious rituals there.

Pearl Bailey

A perfectionist is a man who, if he were married
to Marilyn Monroe, would expect her to cook.

Milton Berle

Everyone keeps asking if Tiger Woods has
a weakness. He has: he can't cook.

Bernard Langer

There's one thing more exasperating than
a wife who can cook and won't and that's
the wife who can't cook and will.

Robert Frost

Never trust a thin cook.

Charlotte Wright

My prowess in the kitchen is confined
to making minestrone soup.

Bryan Forbes

Cooking is like love. It should be entered
into with abandon or not at all.

Harriet van Horne

Cookery without meat is like *Macbeth* without murder.

A.A. Gill

To barbecue is a way of life rather than
a desirable method of cooking.

Clement Freud

If your cooking is as bad as mine,
train your family to eat fast.

Phyllis Diller

My cooking isn't cordon bleu. It's cordon noir.

Phyllis Diller

I was 32 when I started cooking. Up until then I just ate.

Julia Child

Men like to barbecue;
men will cook if danger is involved.

Rita Rudner

My mother viewed being fat as only marginally
better than having an attack of leprosy. She felt it
would render you unmarriable. But I don't see the
point of wasting time at the gym and doing all
those nips and tucks that women of my
age do. I'd rather be cooking up a storm,
drinking red wine and behaving badly.

Erin Pizzey

Kissing don't last, cooking do.

George Meredith

I miss my wife's cooking – as often as I can.

Henny Youngman

I like white trash cooking: cheeseburgers, the greasier
the better; mashed potatoes served in a scoop, a little
dent in the top for the gravy; Drake's Devil Dogs
for dessert. Pure pleasure; no known nutrient.

Orson Bean

When men reach their sixties and retire they go
to pieces. Women just go right on cooking.

Gail Sheehy

I killed my first wife because she undercooked my
steak and my second because she overcooked it.

*Frenchman Noel Carriou in 1973. He escaped the charge
of murder, the presiding judge emphasising the fact that
'The quality of cooking is an important part of marriage' before
sending him down for eight years for manslaughter*

I once toyed with the idea of doing a cookbook. I think
a lot of people who hate literature but love fried
eggs would have bought it if the price was right.

Groucho Marx

All the world's top chefs are men,
so the question I want to ask is:
how come most of them claim they can't cook?

Diana Dors

I can never understand the success
of cookery programmes on TV.
I can't smell it, can't taste it, can't eat it.
At the end of the show they say to the camera,
'Well, here it is. You can't have any. Goodbye.'

Jerry Seinfeld

8

Meals

A man is in general better pleased when he has a good
dinner upon his table than when his wife talks Greek.

Samuel Johnson

A man seldom thinks with more earnestness
of anything than he does of his dinner.

Samuel Johnson

All happiness depends on a leisurely breakfast.

John Gunter

The crunch period in matrimony is breakfast time.

A.P. Herbert

My favourite meal is breakfast, lunch,
dinner and in-between.

Totie Fields

When my mother had to get dinner for eight,
she'd make enough for sixteen and only serve half.

Gracie Allen

Whenever I sit down to a meal I always make a point
of leaving just four inches between my stomach
and the edge of the table. When I feel them rubbing
together pretty hard, I know I've had enough.

*Celebrated nineteenth century gourmand James
'Diamond Jim' Brady. New York restaurateur Charles
Rector described him as 'the best 25 customers we had'.*

The beneficent effects of the regular quarter hour's
exercise before breakfast is more than offset by the
mental wear and tear in getting out of bed fifteen
minutes earlier than one otherwise would.

Simeon Strunsky

The most remarkable thing about my mother is
that for 30 years she served nothing but leftovers.
The original meal was never found.

Tracey Ullman

I diet between meals.

Michael Winner

I'm a man more dined against than dining.

Sir Maurice Bowra

Bill Clinton's foreign policy experience
stemmed mainly from having had breakfast
at the International House of Pancakes.

Pat Buchanan

I diet very strenuously. First I have breakfast, then diet.
Then I have lunch, followed by a light diet in order to
prepare for afternoon tea, which should be followed by
a fair amount of dieting until dinner time. If the system
can stand it, one should fast from then until supper.

Lennie Lower

When I was a child, the family menu consisted
of two choices: take it or leave it.

Buddy Hackett

When you have children your meal intake
goes from two a day to fourteen. Then there
are the extra ones you fish out of the bin.

Jo Brand

By six years of age I was a fatso who finished her
midnight snack just in time for breakfast.

Joan Rivers

My biggest decision in life is whether to put salt or pepper
on my eggs in the morning. I'm too lazy to shake both.

Orson Welles

Journalists often ask how much I weigh.
I tell them, 'Only once a day, before breakfast.'

Les Dawson

I only have three meals a day.
But breakfast lasts from 8 to 12, dinner from
1 to 5 and tea from 6 until midnight.

John Candy

The worst thing about having a mistress
is those two dinners you have to eat.

Oscar Levant

You know you've had too much to eat for Christmas
dinner when you slump down onto a beanbag and
realise you haven't slumped down onto a beanbag.

David Letterman

I've been on the Slimfast diet. For breakfast you have
a shake. For lunch you have a shake. For dinner
you kill anyone with food on their plate.

Rosie O'Donnell

After a good dinner one can forgive
anybody, even one's own relations.

Oscar Wilde

Women have a right to work wherever and
whenever they want to, so long as they have
the dinner ready when you get home.

John Wayne

The soccer player Fatty Foulke once sat down
to lunch early and ate the food intended for the
whole team and for the opposition too.

William Donaldson

I have to go now, Clarice.
I'm having an old friend for dinner.

Anthony Hopkins as Hannibal Lecter
in The Silence of the Lambs

Ask your child what he wants for
dinner only if he's buying.

Fran Lebowitz

My kids keep trying to convince me that there
are two separate parts of their stomachs,
one dedicated to dinner and the other to dessert.

Anna Quindlen

Sundays in France are strange affairs. It's a prolonged
eating day. It's a 'talking among themselves
about what they're about to eat, what they're
eating, and what they've just eaten' day. If you are
not a family member, and not well versed in the
gastronomical nuances of 'une certain sauce' or a
'Coquille Saint-Jacques', then Sunday invitations
to dinner should be avoided. Even in restaurants,
the lone Sunday diner attracts as much attention as
an arsonist, or some such deviant, on his day off.

Mick Hanly

When I was a nurse, my favourite assignment
was the anorexic ward. Sometimes I ate
as many as seventeen dinners.

Jo Brand

The best number for a dinner party is two:
myself and a damn good head waiter.

John Candy

Food gives real meaning to dining-room furniture.

Fran Lebowitz

Ask not what you can do for your
country but what's for lunch.

Orson Welles

At a dinner party one should eat wisely but not
too well and talk well but not too wisely.

W. Somerset Maugham

Robert Morley is a legend in his own lunchtime.

Rex Harrison

Whenever I want a really nice meal I start dating again.

Susan Healy

The Americans spent more money on diet
programmes last year than the total cost of the
National Education Budget. The latest problem over
there in male bulimia. Men today want to look like
what Tom Wolfe called 'social X-rays': in other words
the ladies who lunch. Or rather don't lunch.

John Griffin

There's nothing like a morning funeral
for sharpening the appetite for lunch.

Arthur Marshall

I pray that death will strike me in the middle
of a large meal. I want to be buried under
a tablecloth between four large dishes.

Marc Desaugiers

My stomach rumbles *after* meals.

Charles Laughton

He that looketh on a plate of ham and eggs to lust after it
hath already committed breakfast with it in his heart.

C.S. Lewis

All's well that ends with a good meal.

Arnold Lobel

9

Eating Out and
World Cuisine

The golden rule when reading a menu in a restaurant is,
if you can't pronounce it, you can't afford it.

Frank Muir

Dining out with kids is brilliant. They're the cheapest
dates you'll find. They never order the lobster.

David Letterman

On the continent people have good food.
In England they have good table manners.

George Mikes

The discovery of a new dish does more for the happiness
of mankind than the discovery of a new star.

Jean Anthelme Brillat-Savarin

A gourmet is just a glutton with brains.

Philip Haberman

You don't eat Chinese food. You just rent it.

Jasper Carrott

I don't like French women, French fashion or French
music. But they know how to whip up a plate of grub.

Mike Royko

Americans can eat garbage, provided you sprinkle
it liberally with ketchup, mustard, chilli sauce,
Tabasco sauce, cayenne pepper or any other condiment
which destroys the original flavour of the dish.

Henry Miller

We were taken to a fast food cafe where our order
was fed into a computer. Our hamburgers, made
from the flesh of chemically-impregnated cattle,
had been boiled over counterfeit charcoal, placed
between slices of artificially-flavoured cardboard
and served to us by recycled juvenile delinquents.

Jean-Michel Chapareau

In England we've got 'Eat as much as you like'
restaurants. In America they have 'Eat as much
as you can' ones. They've added an element of
competition. You can be enjoying a delicious
meal and also be going for a personal best.

Jimmy Carr

The French cook, we open tins.

John Galsworthy

If I had my life to live over,
I'd live over a Chinese restaurant.

John Junkin

The French are merely the Germans with good food.

Erma Bombeck

The trouble with eating Italian food is that five
or six days later you're hungry again.

George Miller

The English contribution to world cuisine – the chip.

John Cleese

Nouvelle cuisine roughly translated means,
'I can't believe I just paid $200 and I'm still hungry.'

Mike Kalina

I went to a restaurant that served breakfast 'at any time'.
I ordered French toast during the Renaissance.

Steven Wright

If we should promise people nothing more than
revolution, they would scratch their heads and say,
'Isn't it better to have good goulash?'

Nikita Khrushchev

From experience I know that anything ending in 'os'
on a restaurant menu is pronounced 'heartburn'.

Hugh Leonard

There's no such thing as gourmet coffee,
gourmet rolls or gourmet pizza. Gourmet means
one thing: 'we're going to charge you more'.

George Carlin

The scented flesh of the grouse tasted like an
old courtesan's flesh marinated in a bidet.

Edmond de Goncourt

The food in hospitals is so bad it doesn't
even make it onto airplanes.

Ellen DeGeneres

Ireland was grand. I ate myself daft.

Dylan Thomas

The proof that God has a very weird sense of humour
is that, having invented the sublime mystery of
haute cuisine, he went and gave it to the French.

A.A. Gill

A delicatessen is a shop selling the worst parts of
animals more expensively than the nice parts.

Mike Barfield

Whenever I go to a restaurant
I always ask for a table near the waiter.

Orson Welles

I went to a conference for bulimics and anorexics. It was
a nightmare. The bulimics ate the anorexics. But it was
okay because they were back again in ten minutes.

Monica Piper

There's nothing to do on the Riviera but look at
the view and eat. I do not like to look at the view.

Zelda Fitzgerald

I was polishing off the last mouthful of a dish
in a restaurant when I overheard one waiter
whisper to another, 'He's actually eating it.'

Gilbert Harding

Nouvelle cuisine usually means not enough
on your plate and too much on your bill.

Paul Bocuse

The food in that restaurant is just terrible.
And such small portions.

Woody Allen

I survived a triple bypass operation in 1993 but a
bigger achievement was surviving the hospital food.

Michael Winner

I never go to restaurants with elaborate menus.
They always give you less food.

Jackie Gleason

I don't like dining out because I want outrageously
obscene amounts of food and upscale restaurants
rarely provide this. The quantities I'm referring
to are best found on supermarket shelves.

Janeane Garofalo

If you ask for a doggy bag on a date you might
as well wrap up your genitals too because you're
not going to be needing them for a long time.

Jerry Seinfeld

The average airplane is 16 years old
and so is the average airplane meal.

Joan Rivers

10

Food
and Sex

My favourite sexual fantasy is smearing my
naked body with chocolate and cream and
being left in a room on my own to eat it.

Jo Brand

Anyone who eats three meals a day should understand
why cookbooks outsell sex books three to one.

L.N. Boyd

I have food dreams instead of sex ones.

Rona Jaffe

I'm at the age when food has taken the
place of sex in my life. In fact I've just had
a mirror put over my kitchen table.

Rodney Dangerfield

New York is a lovely, wonderful place to be fat.
Even thin people look fat there, and fat people are always
out with handsome men. New York has fat people the
way fat people should be – happy and healthy and sexy.

Roseanne

Let's face it: if your average woman knew as
much about sexual politics as she does
about the number of calories in a slice of
cheesecake, society would be a matriarchy.

Serena Gray

Apparently eight out of ten women prefer
making love to a fat man. I don't know his
name but he's having a bloody good time.

Andy Hamilton

Great food is like great sex.
The more you have, the more you want.

Gail Greene

I wanted oral sex from my girlfriend but she said
there were too many calories in semen. She didn't
want to put on weight. I told her she'd put on a
lot more if she gave me the other kind of sex.

Charlie Calonne

My idea of perfection is a man who
turns into a pizza after sex.

Leonora Guimard

As life's pleasures go, food is second only to sex.
Except for salami and eggs. That's better than
sex, at least if the salami is sliced thick enough.

Alan King

If I had to choose between sex and food, I'd choose food –
but I'd choose sex over nearly everything else.

Helen Gurley Brown

I'm an Irish Catholic so my father
never discussed women or sex with me.
We talked about sandwich meat instead.

Conan O'Brien

England: The only country in the world where
the food is more dangerous than the sex.

Jackie Mason

Big women have an abundant amount of
sexual fantasies. More so than thin ones.
We pump more oestrogen, so we want it more.

Dawn French

Scientists have discovered a food that reduces a
woman's sex drive by 99 per cent: wedding cake.

Jim Davidson

I haven't trusted polls since I read that 62 per cent of
women had affairs during their lunch hour. I've never
met a woman in my life who would give up food for sex.

Erma Bombeck

Marge, I'd miss you so much if you went away.
Not just for the sex, but also the food preparation.

Homer Simpson

According to a new study, overweight people have a better sex drive than thin people. I think that's because overweight people have to drive a lot further to get sex.

Jay Leno

After a certain age, food is one of the few vices left that you can enjoy. The kids have gone and have their own lives. Your job is a memory. Physical activities are a real effort. A new car no longer gives you the kick it once did. Food is one of the few fantasies you can lust after and turn into reality. It even replaces sex.

Erma Bombeck

I don't feel sexy when I lose weight.

Beyoncé

Fat people are brilliant in bed. If I'm sitting on top of you, are you going to argue?

Jo Brand

Most men secretly fancy large women. They love to sink themselves into softness, to sleep wrapped around curvy hips and swollen bellies, to rest their heads against ample bosoms. They keep their desire a dark secret. They're seen out with a coat-hanger because fashion dictates it.

Dawn French

How do I stay in shape? I eat cotton wool
and sleep with everyone on the planet.

Kate Beckinsale

The trouble with my ex-wife is she was a
whore in the kitchen and a chef in bed.

Groucho Marx

I once had a man break up with me.
He said I was using him because right after
making love I would weigh myself.

Emily Levine

11

Daft
Diets

I'm on this fantastic new diet. You eat whatever you
want, whenever you want, as much as you want to.
You don't lose any weight but it's easy to stick to.

Rodney Dangerfield

Two cannibals were eating a clown.
One said to the other, 'Does this taste funny to you?'

Tommy Cooper

During Prohibition I was forced to live for
days on nothing but food and water.

W.C. Fields

Orson Welles' idea of a balanced diet was
a glass of brandy in each hand.

Chic Murray

Calista Flockhart went on a banana diet.
Now she looks like one.

Geoff Wheaton

I used to eat quite a lot of fast food. When Chelsea
started preschool and she was asked what her
father did, she said he worked at McDonald's.

Bill Clinton

Kids should throw away the cereal and eat the box.
At least that way they'd get some fibre.

Richard Holstein

I tried the Atkins diet once. It gives you dog breath.

Stephen Fry

After Atkins, the latest weight-loss craze is the GI diet.
Actually, there's nothing new here. It was especially
popular among women in Britain during World War II.
It consisted of chocolate, Coca-Cola and, if you
were really lucky, a pair of nylons. Unfortunately,
most women put on the GI diet put on weight.
And it took them nine months to get it off again.

Richard Littlejohn

I'm on a grapefruit diet. I eat everything but grapefruits.

Chi Chi Rodriguez

I'm on a whisky diet. I've lost three days already.

Tommy Cooper

Swallow razor blades if you want to sharpen your appetite.

Janet Rogers

My wife is on a diet. Coconuts and bananas.
She hasn't lost any weight, but can she climb a tree!

Henny Youngman

If you have formed the habit of checking on every new
diet that comes along you will find that, mercifully,
they all blur together, leaving you with only one definite
piece of information: French-fried potatoes are out.

Jean Kerr

I'd have no objection to people who eat like sparrows
if only they'd stop that everlasting chirping about it.

Bob Monkhouse

My idea of a balanced diet is a Big Mac in both hands.

Jackie Gleason

Let me diet eating ortolans to the sound of soft music.

Benjamin Disraeli

Food is an important part of a balanced diet.

Fran Lebowitz

I'm on this new diet which allows me to
eat as much poison as I want. Great.

Tony Francis

I went on a diet but I had to go on another
one at the same time because the first
diet wasn't giving me enough food.

Barry Marter

Liquid diets: the powder is mixed with water and
tastes exactly like powder mixed with water.

Art Buchwald

Smoking eighty cigarettes a day is my only diet plan.

Art Hadleigh

I've been on the Valium diet for 8½ years now.
It doesn't really curb your appetite
but most of your food falls on the floor.

George Miller

The doctor put me on a staple diet
but I find paper clips easier to swallow.

Matthew Brown

My advice if you insist on slimming:
eat as much as you want, just don't swallow it.

Harry Secombe

I tried to exist on vitamins B, C, D and E.
All that happened was I threw up alphabetically.

Les Dawson

Knew a girl who went on a milk diet. She now
weighs fifty-nine quarts and one pint.

Lane Olinghouse

I went on a diet, swore off drinking and heavy eating,
and in fourteen days I lost two weeks.

Joe E. Lewis

I'm on two diets at the moment because
you don't get enough to eat with one.

Peter Sessions

I just gave up caffeine and sugar because I was
feeling sluggish and anxious. Now I have a lot
more energy to feel angry and deprived.

Jennifer Siegal

There's a new dieting invention called the Sniff Diet,
which is an inhaler that smells like Fritos.
When you're hungry you smell it and it tricks your body
into thinking you're eating. Half the people using it are
losing weight. The other half are eating the inhalers.

Tim Bedore

In the matter of diet I have been persistently strict
in sticking to the things that didn't agree with me
until one or the other of us got the best of it.

Mark Twain

I'm on the mirror diet. You eat all your food in front
of a mirror in the nude. It works pretty good, though
some of the fancier restaurants don't go for it.

Roseanne

The French have a superb method for losing
seven pounds immediately – the guillotine.

Les Dawson

12

The Light-Hearted Side
of Weight

I used to have a great big barrel chest,
but that's all behind me now.

Bob Hope

The main reason fat people are so happy is
because we know we've done the wrong
thing and we don't really give a hoot.

Dolly Parton

Abdication means finally giving up on the hope that
one day you're going to have a six-pack stomach.

John Goodman

I'm just short for my weight;
by rights I should measure eight foot three.

Sue Margolis

You know you're getting fat when
you step on the dog's tail and he dies.

Elayne Boosler

From the day she weighs 140 pounds,
the chief excitement in a woman's life is
spotting women who are fatter than she is.

Helen Rowland

According to my girth I should be a ninety-foot redwood.

Erma Bombeck

My husband is almost as heavy as I am.
We were married in adjoining churches.

Roseanne

I'm too skinny. In fact, if it wasn't for my
Adam's apple I'd have no shape at all.

Phyllis Diller

Skinny trends are a fat lot of good.

Siobhan O'Connor

I haven't seen my toes in fifteen years.

Benny Hill

We don't rent bouncy castles at
children's parties. I do it myself.

Roy 'Chubby' Brown

My passport photograph only fits my nose.

Jackie Gleason

I realised I was over weight when my
appendix scar grew to nine inches.

Jackie Gleason

Inside every fat person there's a thin person
looking to get out. They've just eaten them.

Jo Brand

When I got pregnant my mother said to me
'Eating for two, are we?' I replied,
'Yes, but I do that all the time anyway'.

Angie Sinclair

After Simon Raven split with his wife she
telegraphed: 'Wife And Baby Starving'.
He's supposed to have wired back: 'Eat Baby'.

Francis Partridge

Middle age is when your wife tells you to
pull in your stomach, and you already have.

Jack Barry

I comfort myself by pretending that the
number on my bathroom scales is my IQ.

Linda Iverson

I got out of Hastings when I was seventeen ... stone.

Jo Brand

If you hear of sixteen or eighteen pounds of human
flesh, it's mine. I feel as if a curate has been taken out of me.

Sir Sydney Smith after a stringent diet

If I'd been around when Rubens was painting I would
have been revered as a fabulous model. Kate Moss?
Well, she would have been the paintbrush.

Dawn French

A walking X-ray.

Oscar Levant on Audrey Hepburn

I ate more than you weigh for dinner.

Jackie Gleason to a friend

When anorexics look in the mirror they see
someone fat. So I'm an anorexic.

Jo Brand

Always date fat girls. They'll give you shade
in the summer and shelter in the winter.

Joseph Mason

The reason I'm fat is because eating makes me hungry.

Dawn French

I got my first assignment as a director in 1927.
I was slim, arrogant, cocksure, dreamy
and irritating. Today I'm no longer slim.

Michael Powell

I look like a lampshade on legs.

Julia Roberts

I was sunbathing on a beach last summer
and a lifeguard came up to me and said,
'Madam, you'll have to move. The tide wants to come in.'

Marjorie Rea

I don't diet and yet I never put on an ounce.
I eat six meals a day, four steaks, ten pounds of potatoes,
a dozen hamburgers, apple pie, ice cream and lots of
beer. Yet I still weigh the same twenty-eight stone.

Cyril Smith

The diet isn't working when you donate your
liver, kidneys and an arm to lose weight
rather than cut back on your food.

Emma Burgess

I don't mind putting on some weight. I tell people it's just
in case I need to get in character to play the older Elvis.

*Kurt Russell, who portrayed Elvis Presley
in* Elvis: The Movie

I'm still the same as I always was –
fat, out of shape, all the good stuff.

John Daly

When your daughter hands her maternity dresses on
to you and you're 55 it's time to think about a diet.

Peter Grey

Don't be misled by weighing scales. They're the most
lying things on earth and should be treated accordingly.
When you see sixteen stone ten pounds on the dial,
think of the number you first thought of and stick to it.

Lennie Lower

She knew it was time to shed a few pounds
when it took three waiters and a forklift to
give her the Heimlich manoeuvre.

Cindy Adams

My tailor has three sizes:
Small, medium, and 'It's him again'.

Roscoe 'Fatty' Arbuckle

I tried on last year's suit. The only thing that
still fitted me was the handkerchief.

Rodney Dangerfield

Success has gone to my stomach.

Michael Winner

My tailor uses an elastic measuring tape.

Burl Ives

My mother is so fat, when she gets on
the scale it says, 'To Be Continued'.

Damon Wayans

I'm not the stuff that heroes are made from.
I'm too scared to fight and too fat to run.

Les Dawson

The last time I got stuck in a revolving door
it took me three hours to get out.

Victor Buono

As I rose from the bath I looked in the mirror
and saw a great white sea monster emerging
out of the water. This enormous sub-aquatic
creature could not possibly be me, could it?

Julian Fellowes

The reason people stick in their stomachs when they
weigh themselves is so they can see the scales.

Maria Chaves

My bum has frequently caused eclipses of the sun.

Jo Brand

You know you're too heavy when you bend down
to tie your shoelaces and your tits get there first.

Rosie O'Donnell

When I wake up in the morning and look in the
mirror I realise that one of the reasons I don't own a
handgun is, I would have shot my thighs off years ago.

Oprah Winfrey

I have flabby thighs but fortunately
my stomach covers them.

Shelley Winters

The only reason I've been called the strong silent type is because I find it difficult to talk to women when I'm trying to hold my stomach in.

Pat Ingoldsby

The diet isn't working when you're the only person in the weight loss programme ... because there isn't room for anyone else.

Emma Burgess

I used to go to a restaurant where you could eat as much as you wanted for a given fee. They closed down.

Harry Secombe

The diet isn't working if the fire brigade calls you out to act as a human shield whenever someone threatens to jump off a high building.

Emma Burgess

One thing my mother could never say to me was, 'Your eyes are bigger than your belly.'

Brendan Grace

We have women in the military but they don't know if we can kill. I think we can. All the general has to do is walk over to the women and say 'You see the enemy over there? They say you look fat in those uniforms.'

Elayne Boosler

You know the diet isn't working when
your arse needs its own passport.

Emma Burgess

It's time to go on a diet when Prudential
offers you Group Insurance.

Totie Fields

I hate orgies. You have to hold your
stomach in for hours on end.

Billy Connolly

Anorexia is just another word for nothing left to lose.

Joy Behar

I am not overweight. I'm just nine inches too short.

Shelley Winters

If someone calls me fat I don't get angry.
I just turn the other chin.

Jo Brand

What do you mean I'm out of shape? Round is a shape.

Jackie Gleason

The only thing I would change in my life is my bottom.
With two other women.

Jennifer Lopez

The best way to look thin is to hang out with people
fatter than yourself. In my face this is not easy.

Shelley Winters

When the scales revealed that I had put on weight,
my 'gut' reaction was to call it a lying bastard.

Maurice Neligan

Her heart is in the right place.
It's a pity the other fifteen stone isn't.

Cows, I read somewhere, have four stomachs.
I think I must have been a cow in a previous life.

Victor Buono

I once got stuck in the revolving door of a hotel.
The porter told me to try backing out sideways.
'Honey,' I said, 'I ain't got no sideways'.

Bernice Rubens

I have the opposite of anorexia. I think I'm thin. I'm in
a support group. We all sit around in skin-tight
clothing going, 'Is this too baggy to wear?'

Caroline Rhea

I'm happy to say I lost weight after the baby.
Of course, it took me four years. And we adopted.

Andrea Henry

I try my best to diet but the fat still sticks
out through the holes in my vest.

Roy 'Chubby' Brown

When I was young everything I ate went instantly to
my thighs, like a squirrel storing food in its cheeks.

Joan Rivers

The diet isn't working when a local entrepreneur
applies for planning permission to build
a ski-slope on your double chin.

Emma Burgess

Bob Monkhouse

I wasn't being free with my hands.
I was trying to guess her weight.

W.C. Fields

Weight Watchers Meeting At 7 p.m.
Please Use The Large Double Doors.

Notice outside church

I went on to one of those 'Speak Your Weight'
machines. It said, 'Promise you won't get violent'.

Jackie Gleason

I won't tell you how much I eat, but don't get in an
elevator with me unless you're going down.

Jack E. Leonard

I've gained and lost the same ten pounds so many times
over and over again, my cellulite must have deja vu.

Jane Wagner

I'm two years ahead on my daily fat allowance.
I'm looking for skinny people to see if I can borrow theirs.

Jo Brand

Obesity is a fat accompli

Len Elliott

You know you're fat when you can't get into
the bath at the same time as the water.

Rodney Dangerfield

I dropped a few pounds last week.
They landed around my knees.

Louis Anderson

I've gained a few pounds around the middle.
The only lower-body garments I own that
still fit me comfortably are towels.

Dave Barry

With my bum size, décolletage is my only hope.
The theory is that men will be so mesmerised by
my cleavage that they won't notice my bum.

Jane Owen

When I open a refrigerator door nothing is
safe, not even the pipes.

Marlon Brando

Does 'flabbergasted' mean being disgusted
over all the weight you've put on?

Victoria Wood

Beer doesn't make you fat.
It makes you lean –
against tables, chairs, poles ...

Graffiti

I started smoking to lose weight.
After I dropped that lung I felt pretty good.

Michael Meehan

You can tell you ate too much for Christmas
when you have to let your kaftan out.

Rosie O'Donnell

As a girl I wanted to be an air hostess because
people don't finish their meals on planes and I could
scoff everything left behind the secret curtains.

Dawn French

I don't have an hourglass figure.
I have an hour and a half.

Wendy Liebman

I have a weight of twenty stone squeezed into a five foot
eight inch frame as a result of having been hit by a lift.

Harry Secombe

I'm an expert on losing weight.
I represent the survival of the fattest.

Alfred Hitchcock

I have more folds than an origami convention.

Roscoe 'Fatty' Arbuckle

I'm on a diet as my skin doesn't fit me anymore.

Erma Bombeck

You can say what you like about long dresses
but they cover a multitude of shins.

Mae West

By six years of age I ate so much I had
stretch marks around my mouth.

Joan Rivers

His wife used to have a nice firm chin,
but now the firm has taken on a couple of partners.

George Coote

I tried burning off the fat.
It cost me a fortune in matches.

Les Dawson

I've got my figure back after giving birth.
I was hoping to get someone else's.

Caroline Quentin

You know it's time to go on a diet when you're standing
next to your car and get a ticket for double parking.

Totie Fields

If you throw a sandwich off the Empire State Building,
it gathers enough speed to crack the pavement. I know,
because I saw one coming down once and tried to catch it.

Jo Brand

As accurately as I can calculate, between the ages
of 10 and 70 I have eaten forty-four wagon-loads
of food more than was good for me.

Sydney Smith

The only thing about me that's getting
thinner these days is my hair.

Shelley Winters

I was never the type to go on a Fat Pride walk as
a child. I was more likely to write a Fat Apology letter.

Roseanne

When we played football at school I was always
put in goal, basically because I filled most of it.

Janet Bryant

13

Food
Philosophy

There's no bore more boring than the slimming bore.

Peter Dobereiner

You don't get ulcers from what you eat.
You get them from what's eating you.

Vicki Baum

I've learned not to put things in
my mouth that are bad for me.

*Monica Lewinsky on Larry King's chat show in a
discussion about weight loss, not oral sex*

The verb 'To diet' can only be conjugated in the
future tense, as in, 'I will diet, you will diet, etc.'

Michael Harkness

When people say to me less is more,
I reply 'More is more'.

Dolly Parton

I eat merely to put food out of my mind.

N.F. Simpson

I never eat when I can dine.

Maurice Chevalier

I stay away from natural foods.
At my age I need all the preservatives I can get.

George Burns

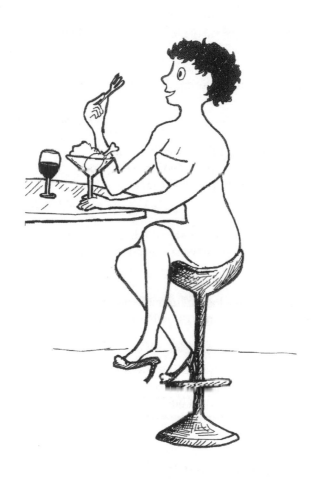

The only way to get rid of temptation is to yield to it.

Oscar Wilde

Practise safe eating. Use condiments.

Jasper Carrott

There's something I've noticed about food:
whenever there's a crisis, if you can get people
to eat, normally things get better.

Madeleine L'Engle

Seize the moment. Remember all those women
who waved aside the dessert tray on the *Titanic*.

Erma Bombeck

If you are ever at a loss to support a flagging
conversation, introduce the subject of eating.

Leigh Hunt

Great restaurants are nothing but mouth brothels.
There's no point in going to them if one
intends to keep one's belt buckled.

Frederic Raphael

To eat is human, to digest divine.

Charles Copeland

Be content to remember that those who can
make omelettes properly can do nothing else.

Hilaire Belloc

Always serve too much hot fudge sauce
on hot fudge sundaes. It makes people
overjoyed, and puts them in your debt.

Judith Olney

Terror is the only word for facing a day with
only 800 calories: black, ugly terror.

Helen Gurley Brown

Better to be remembered as a jolly old soul
than a depressed dieter.

Fern Britton

A restaurant is the only place in the world
where people are happy to be fed up.

Hal Roach

If God meant us to eat peanut butter
he would have given us Teflon gums.

Robert Orpen

You don't have to lay an egg to know if it tastes good.

Pauline Kael

Love never dies of starvation, but often of indigestion.

Ninon de Lenclos

Eat, drink and be merry, for tomorrow ye diet.

William Gilmour

If you eat the right food all the time you'll die healthy.

Anon

A diet is an all-consuming obsession with the food
you shouldn't have eaten yesterday but did, the food
you have eaten today but shouldn't have, and the
food you shouldn't eat tomorrow but probably will.

Sandra Bergson

Thou shalt not weigh more than thy refrigerator.

John Goodman

Anything you have to acquire a taste
for wasn't meant to be eaten.

Eddie Murphy

Life is too short to stuff a mushroom.

Shirley Conran

Don't marry on an empty stomach.

John Travolta

The best way to lose weight is to put the handle
of the fridge two inches from the ground.

Dawn French

I'm not a glutton; I'm an explorer of food.

Erma Bombeck

A health addict is someone who eats health food so
he won't ruin his health and have to eat health food.

Hal Roach

I don't believe in diets. Every time I come off them
I eat double to make up for all the time I wasted.

Rodney Dangerfield

It's not true I eat like a pig.
I just suffer from reverse bulimia.

Dawn French

No man in the world has more courage than
the one who can stop eating after one peanut.

Stuart Turner

I'm a light eater. As soon as it's light, I start eating.

Brendan Grace

A really busy person never knows how much he weighs.

Edgar Watson Howe

No matter how fat you are, buy your
clothes a size too big. That way people
actually think you're trimming down.

Les Sterling

Thomas Jefferson wrote, 'We never repent
of having eaten too little.' What a load of
nonsense some people come out with.

Maurice Neligan

I like the word 'indolence'.
It makes my laziness seem classy.

Bern Williams

I've decided to cut out eating on days
that don't have a 'Y' in them.

Jo Brand

I eat when I'm depressed and I eat when I'm happy. When
I can't decide whether I'm depressed or happy,
I make the decision while I'm eating.

Oprah Winfrey

The second day of a diet is always easier than
the first because by then you're off it.

Jackie Gleason

Dieticians are the worst enemies of great cuisine.
It is impossible to have low calories in excellent food.

Louis Vaudable

If you lose weight to keep your ass, your face goes.
But if the face is good, your ass isn't. I'll choose the face.

Kathleen Turner

The best way to prevent sagging as you grow
older is to keep eating till the wrinkles fill out.

John Candy

Why do people say 'You just want to have your
cake and eat it'? What's the point of having
a cake unless you're going to eat it?

Billy Connolly

Can you imagine a world without men?
There'd be no crime, and lots of fat happy women.

Nicole Hollander

Overeating is the most worthy of sins.
It neither breaks up marriages
nor causes any accidents.

Richard Gordon

Part of the secret of success in life is to eat what
you want and let the food fight it out inside.

Mark Twain

Never serve oysters in a month
that has no pay cheque in it.

P.J. O'Rourke

Have you ever noticed that jewels make a woman
either incredibly fat or incredibly thin?

J.M. Barrie

Cigarette sales would drop to zero overnight
if the warning said, 'This packet contains fat'.

Dave Barry

You could probably get through life without knowing
how to roast a chicken but would you want to?

Nigella Lawson

Never share credit – or desserts.

Beverly Sills

So much food, so little time.

Caryl Avery

I always eat dessert first because life is so uncertain.

Robert Morley

The best anti-ageing cream is ice cream.
What other food makes you feel like
you're eight years old again?

Howard Dietz

A highbrow is someone who looks at a
sausage and thinks of Picasso.

A.P. Herbert

If you ask a hungry man how much is
two and two, he replies, 'Four loaves'.

Hindu proverb

A man of sixty has spent twenty years
in bed and over three years eating.

Alan Bennett

A man who refuses apple dumplings
cannot have a good conscience.

Charles Lamb

The first thing I remember liking
that liked me back was food.

Valerie Harper

An optimist is someone on Death Row
who's also a member of Weight Watchers.

Jonathan Katz

If you think the way to a man's heart is
through his stomach, you're aiming too high.

June Rogers

There's nothing worse than being stuck up in the
Andes after a plane crash with your anorexic buddy.

Denis Leary

The reason I got so fat is because, having created
objective art as a young man, as time went on
I resolved to create a subjective work of art – myself.

Orson Welles

War is cannibalism while dieting.

Leonard Levinson

The only time a man likes to see a woman
overweight is if she's a woman he nearly married.

Oliver Herford

The fate of a nation has often depended on
the good or bad digestion of a Prime Minister.

Voltaire

Gluttony is not a secret vice.

Orson Welles

Remember, you're all alone in the
kitchen and no one can see you.

Julia Child

All the talk going round about the high cost of living
is just propaganda put about by people who eat.

Jay Leno

I don't take soup. You can't build a meal on a lake.

Lady Mendl

Where you eat is sacred.

Mel Brooks

I don't believe in dining on an empty stomach.

W.C. Fields

Age does not diminish the extreme disappointment
of having a scoop of ice cream fall from the cone.

Jim Freiberg

Weighing scales are usually accurate, but seldom tactful.

Bill Cosby

People often feed the hungry so that they
won't disturb them while they're eating.

Somerset Maugham

The trouble about playing golf away from home
is you eat fast food. It's better when you play local.
That way you can bring the fast food home with you.

Gary McCord

Choose your companions carefully –
you may have to eat them.

W.C. Sellar

In the Middle Ages they had stretch racks, guillotines,
whips and chains. Nowadays we have a much more
effective torture device: the bathroom scale.

Stephen Phillips

When women get depressed they eat or go shopping.
Men invade countries.

Elayne Boosler

I love the Chinese greeting.
They can't say 'Hello'.
They say 'Have you eaten yet?'

Rick Stein

There is no love sincerer than the love of food.

George Bernard Shaw

Why is it that all the things I really like eating have
been proven to cause tumours in white mice?

Robert Benchley

Seeing isn't believing.
It's eating that's believing.

James Thurber

A recipe is a series of step-by-step instructions
for preparing ingredients you forgot to buy,
in utensils you don't own, to make a
dish the dog won't eat the rest of.

Henry Beard

Never accept an invitation from a stranger
unless he offers you candy.

Linda Festa

Broken biscuits are calorie-free.
The process of breaking causes calorie leakage.

Maurice Silver

Birthdays are nature's way of telling us to eat more cake.

Jo Brand

Grub first, then ethics.

Bertolt Brecht

I always buy suits that are too small for me. Then when
they don't fit, I don't feel obliged to go on a diet.

Gene Perret

It's important to watch what you eat.
Otherwise how are you going to get it into your mouth?

Matt Diamond

If I cook enough spaghetti for Sicily, no one shows,
but if I reheat two small leftover pieces of
pizza they fly in from out of state.

Erma Bombeck

Don't tell your friends about your indigestion.
'How are you' is a greeting, not a question.

Arthur Guiterman

Don't let love interfere with your appetite.

Anthony Trollope

A boy doesn't have to go to war to be a hero. He can say
he doesn't like pie when there isn't enough to go around.

E.W. Howe

Sometimes I think more creativity is put into muffin
recipes than into the rest of society combined.

Jerry Seinfeld

A gourmet who thinks of calories is like
a tart who looks at her watch.

James Beard

If you want to find out some things about yourself
in vivid detail, try calling your wife fat.

P.J. O'Rourke

Napoleon said an army marches on its stomach.
They couldn't have travelled very fast in that position.

Gwen Pollard

Each year a healthy male bore consumes 1½ times
his own weight in other people's patience.

John Updike

All the things I really like to do are either
illegal, immoral or fattening.

Alexander Woolcott

If you enjoyed this book, you may also be interested in …

1916 & All That

C.M. BOYLAN

This wonderfully irreverent take on the history of Ireland. It will take you from the 'Age of the Third Best Metal', through the struggles of Wolfe Tone (Ireland's best-named revolutionary), right through the Celtic Tiger years, when there was pancetta and rubies for all. And then on to the present day, when there are fewer rubies. And, on the way, this book is not afraid to ask the hard questions, such as: Why were walls so important for the Normans? And can you describe and explain Limerick?

978 1 84588 749 0

It's Great to be Back on Terra Cotta

AUBREY MALONE

A hilarious compendium of witticisms for the hardened traveller to savour, from thought-provoking apercus to laugh-out-loud observations on the muted joys of getting from A to B – or NOT getting there, as the case may be. Illustrated with funny cartoons, this handy pocket-sized book by successful collector of witticisms Aubrey Malone is a must-have for any transport enthusiast or seasoned traveller.

978 0 7524 5894 6

Visit our website and discover thousands of other History Press books.

www.thehistorypress.co.uk